THE ART OF Exotic Dancing FOR EVERYDAY WOMEN™

THIS IS A CARLTON BOOK

This edition published by
Carlton Books Limited 2003
20 Mortimer Street
London W1T 3JW

Library of Congress data to come

ISBN 1 84222 899 4

Editorial Manager: Judith More
Art Director: Penny Stock
Production: Lisa Moore

Design and editorial:
Queen's Park Press Ltd
20 Lonsdale Road, London NW6 6RD

Art Director: Chrissie Lloyd
Managing Editor: Antonia Cunningham
Designer: Thomas Keenes
Photographer: Jules Selmes

The author and publisher have made every effort to ensure that all information is correct and up to date at the time of publication. Neither the author nor the publisher can accept responsibility for any accident, injury or damage that results from using the ideas, information or advice offered in this book.

In the interests of good health it is always important to consult your physician before commencing any exercise program, especially if you have a medical condition or are pregnant. All guidelines and warnings should be read carefully. The author and publisher disclaim any liability or loss, personal or otherwise, resulting from the procedures and information in this book.

Printed and bound in Italy.

THE ART OF Exotic Dancing FOR EVERYDAY WOMEN™

Leah Stauffer

CARLTON
BOOKS

Contents

Introduction

The *Art of Exotic Dancing for Everyday Women™* is all about *you* finding *you*. Exotic dance is much more than sexy dancing; it's about learning to reach deep within yourself to find your inner beauty and grace and combine them into sensual routines only you can express. It gives you a chance to reconnect with your creative self through movement. This form of self-empowerment is an experience you'll not quickly forget! The non-intimidating style and breakdown of each routine fosters confidence and self-expression.

THE ART OF EXOTIC DANCING FOR EVERYDAY WOMEN™

We bring you The Art of Exotic Dancing for Everyday Women™ to give you direct access to your own power, beauty, and grace.Discover your most sensual self and increase your confidence in expressing this side of yourself. In today's environment of magazines and television, it is ever-challenging to focus on what you have to offer as opposed to comparing yourself to what you see in those images. If we all had professional hair and make-up artists, great lighting packages, and brilliant photographers to follow us around all day, we too would look like the glitzy pictures we see plastered everywhere. The reality is, however, that we are regular women with regular lives—but it is also that beauty, sensuality, and power are characteristics that each and every one of us possess. Exotic dancing gives you access to these features.

This book is for you and me, us, the "regular" women of the world, mothers, wives, daughters, sisters, friends—the women with careers and responsibilities, all out there shopping, cooking dinner, chauffeuring the kids, and managing our households. I want to say that The Art of Exotic Dancing for Everyday Women™ is written for all of us hot, sexy, beautiful women, but I'm afraid many of us do not see ourselves this way. If the cover of this book stated that it was for the hot and sexy women of the world, would you have ever picked it up? Hopefully, by the time you're done reading this book, you'll be seeing yourself in just that way. Hot, beautiful and very, very sexy. The use of the title

TAMMY, 31

Tammy used "Exotic Dancing" to get past fears instilled in her due to her strict Mennonite upbringing. She says, "This was a great way for me to become comfortable with my sexuality. I always felt very passionately about my sexuality but never had a safe way to express it."

As a child Tammy was not allowed to wear dresses with hemlines above the knee and she also felt intimidated by other womens' sensuality. To take the exotic dance class and be a part of the video was a huge step for her. Taking the class helped her to realize that "It's okay to be yourself and it's okay to move your body however you want to move your body. The classes started to break down walls for me. I am now more accepting of myself and others."

She felt completely supported by the other women in the class and the expression of the lovely woman that she is was welcomed by everybody. She found improved relationships with other women, greater self-esteem and much more self-confidence.

"I got out of the experience so much more than I could ever have imagined. Throughout the process of becoming more comfortable and confident with myself, I have had amazing things happen for me both personally and professionally."

The experience has had such an impact on her that she teaches other women the skills that they can gain through the techniques of The Art of Exotic Dancing for Everyday Women™ experience. She is now showing others how to empower themselves and take hold of their lives for themselves! In fact Tammy got so involved with her dancing that she choreographed a fitness workout, StripFit™ (see pp.98-103), based on the core movements in The Art of Exotic Dancing for Everyday Women™ and is writing a motivational book based loosely on her life experiences.

"The Art of Exotic Dancing for Everyday Women™", as opposed to "How to Exotic Dance" or "Exotic Dancing Made Easy" is deliberate because developing your own dance routines and finding your body's natural rhythms is comparable to the creation of art. Your dance is like a beautiful piece of art. There is no right or wrong way to exotic dance. Your dance is unique to you. In this book, we provide you with the basic moves for your dance but the expression of those moves is yours alone.

The word 'art' is defined as the process of creating of a thing of beauty. The concept of something being a work of art is the uniqueness it embodies. The works of Monet are one of a kind. There are no other like them. While you can try to recreate a picture of water lilies on a pond, they will never look the way they did through Monet's eyes. The light, shadowing, and color expressed through the eyes of the artist. The 'art' of a great chef, winemaker, gardener, or writer cannot be replicated. The expression of yourself through your dance is similarly unique. The flair you bring to a meal is one of a kind. The way you dress, talk, and decorate your home is like no-one else's. Sure it may resemble or emulate another's style—we may strive for that, but no matter how much we try, it is still *our* personalities that shine through. What I hope to convey through this book is that your sensuality, and your expression of it, is at its most beautiful and artistic when it is expressing exactly who you are. Through exotic dancing, we will give you the tools to bring those elements out. There is no-one else like you. You are a gift that you can give to others and to the world, should you choose to do so.

The Art of Exotic Dancing for Everyday Women™ is simply another medium in which to express yourself. Cooking, decorating your home, raising your children, exercising, working, writing, eating, and even breathing are all uniquely done. These daily activities are all expressions of who we are. Exotic dancing is just one more way to express who we are. It is more challenging than some of the everyday things we do but this book provides everything you need to give it all you've got.

I will give you the tools to be confident enough to master the art of exotic dancing. You will learn how to access your power as a woman and use it in healthy, positive ways. You will awaken your sensuality and learn how to express it, anytime, anywhere. You will have fun and depending how often you practise your moves, you will get fit in the process. The way you work, handle people, view others, and the entire way you live will be changed by your courage to try something new. My hope in sharing what I've learned through exotic dancing is to give you another set of tools to take on your life, another set of paint brushes to stroke the canvas.

In this book, I give you the fundamentals of the dance (which are the easy bits) and more importantly, enable you to find a path back to you. For some of you, it may be the first time you ever experience the real you. I want you to feel safe and comfortable expressing yourself and to provide a framework for you to fall in love with yourself. I want you to experience in your body what it feels like to feel sensual. You may not choose to share yourself through dance with anyone, but if you've discovered or been re-introduced to an aspect of yourself that you never knew or had long forgotten, I will have achieved my vision for this book.

THE MAGIC CIRCLE

There is something magical that happens during a class in The Art of Exotic Dancing for Everyday Women™ and it cannot be overlooked in this book. The challenge I face in explaining it to you is how to take something that is transformational in nature and describe it on the pages of a book. This experience is called The Circle, and it is one of the most powerful parts of the exotic-dance experience. First, I'll share with you what The Circle is and how it works. Next, I'll tackle the challenging part, creating the space for you to experience The Circle.

WHAT IS THE CIRCLE?

The Circle is the first thing that happens in the class. It is the first step towards a breakthrough. Women often begin class feeling nervous, anxious or unsure of what to expect. The Circle is how we create a safe space for one another to get to the heart of the matter, which is enabling you to be you. It becomes a safe, almost sacred space in which women can share in a non-judgmental environment. You can share anything and everything, from why you are taking the class or purchasing the video or this book to feelings about your weight, family, job, illnesses, inhibitions, fears, hopes, and desires.

Experience being your real self, show what you feel, and have the opportunity to express it. See what it feels like to be accepted unconditionally by others without having to be the perfect wife, mother, business woman, or friend. Transforming feelings of anxiety, jealousy, competitiveness, embarrassment, shame, and insecurity into positive feelings prepares you for the feelings and sensations that can arise when you dance.

The courage of sharing during The Circle gives us the experience to draw on if these feelings arise during our dance or in any area of our lives. Knowing that we have the power to change our thoughts and emotions feels good and builds our confidence. The amazing part is that we come to realize we have always had this power and now know we always hold the key to access our power and transform thoughts and feelings that prevent us from fully expressing, and therefore fully experiencing, our lives.

HOW IT WORKS

It's so simple, yet so rare. It's why we love Oprah. If you don't like Oprah, let me share with you why many women do. It is the space she has created for authentic sharing. She does it, her guests do it, and her audience does it. It resonates because it is real. She is real and the space she creates for others allows them to be real. The Circle is like that. You get REAL. You feel the most of who you are. You uncover, discover, and re-discover. Have you ever bonded instantly with someone? Have you ever seen two little girls play together? Do you remember your first best friend? Do you remember the feeling of just being you, saying and doing anything? There was no caution, no worry of judgment. You could completely be yourself. That is what the space of The Circle feels like.

We have held classes and sold videos to women from London to California and many stops in-between. I have been in hundreds of classes and received thousands of e-mails from women all over that have shared some powerful transformations. They have moved and inspired me to write this book and consequently have helped us to bring

MOLLY, 40

Molly, a stay-at-home mother of four, took the class with the intention of spicing up her 17-year marriage. She found the class to be "...fun for my husband, but a lot more fun for me." The class helped Molly get over many of her insecurities. She was raised Catholic and believed that sensuality was spoken of in hushed tones. She lost part of herself in the chaos of life.

Molly made a bold step and took an exotic dance class. Through the class she learned how to be confident, discovered all that she is capable of, and realized that it is okay to be sensual and sexy.

Now she teaches classes all over the US and in London. She allows women to be sexy again. "I am delighted that I impact on women by sharing my experience, teaching them sexy moves, and helping them to see that sexuality is something to be celebrated, not be ashamed of."

Her husband says: "Molly came home from the first class and she was on cloud nine ... I hadn't seen her this charged since the birth of our first child."

CATHIE, 54

As a mother, grandmother, and wife of an executive, 54 year-old Cathie felt she was losing her identity. When she was told by a friend that she needed to "slow down" and start wearing long skirts as she was reaching the "mature" stage of her life, Cathie refused to adhere to this advice. Instead she signed up for an exotic dancing class and got involved with making the video. What she learned was how to be less inhibited, how to be a little more sensuous, and that it is okay to be vulnerable and show her vulnerability. She has learned to break down walls by not being afraid of being in her own skin and to be comfortable with herself at all ages. In addition she now has also some great dance routines under her belt and feels completely at ease performing for her partner and sometimes just for herself. "I realized that we all have these feelings of wanting to be beautiful and sexy at any age and that all women are very much alike. I learned how to be a little bit more sensuous and not to be afraid of being a woman and being feminine."

transformation through movement to women all over the world. Their stories and circumstances may vary but the underlying feelings they share are many times the same. With the permission of some of these women, I wanted to bring you a few of the experiences women have had with The Circle and the class. I think you'll recognize some of their feelings in yourself. My hope is that you feel a connection so you have the opportunity to experience a glimpse of what The Circle is all about.

MAKING BREAKTHROUGHS

There is a correlation between the freedom and self-expression of your dance and the freedom and self-expression you convey in your everyday life. Breakthroughs you have in life or through your dance will impact directly on one another. You may begin thinking about areas of your life that you want to change. As you begin dancing, notice times you feel inhibited. Is there some area of your life you want to change? The breakthrough may be about your weight, your beauty, your sensuality, or sexiness, or it may even be in an area not apparently directly related to this book at all. It could be in the way you relate to your family or your co-workers. It may be a breakthrough in how you feel when you walk into a restaurant or ask for directions, or even something as simple as declining an invitation or a favor someone is asking of you.

This part of the book is about you getting a better picture of you. What you like, what you don't, what you desire, how you feel, who you are, and for many women the biggest issue—how to speak your truth? In the areas where your self-expression through dance gets blocked, you will notice that any personal breakthroughs you have will free up your dancing and you will be better able to express who you are. The fuller your expression of yourself, the sexier, more sensual, and more beautiful you will look. This takes courage and for most of us it is stretching outside of our comfort zone. That is why we break it down for you so you can take small or large steps towards a new, more powerful you. Take the steps you are comfortable with—you choose the pace.

The flip side of this is that you feel this section of the book is "not your thing." Interesting, maybe, but really for other people. Do me this favor. Remember this section and return to it when you get stuck in your dancing. Just as personal breakthroughs can cause your dancing to free up, you will find that when something in your dancing feels uncomfortable or completely out of your comfort zone, these are clues as to exactly where your soul is saying, "Area for change, area for breakthrough!" Notice it and if you are up for it, come back and revisit this section from a different perspective.

The bottom line is this: It doesn't matter how you come to it, through dance or head first, we can all use breakthroughs in our life. Transformation not only pushes our lives on, it pushes the planet on. I know it sounds crazy to say that exotic dancing is some big contribution to the world. Well, I'm here to tell you it is. Anything that opens us, expands us, and frees us from worry, judgments, and criticisms to create tolerance and acceptance is a contribution to the work, family, and community relationships in our lives. Our self-expansion, freedom, and acceptance are paths that lead to genuine self-expression. Honest self-expression is a gift we each can give to the world. It will manifest itself in a myriad of ways and we will leave our mark. Our time spent here will have mattered. Okay, again, through exotic dancing? Yes. Are there other ways to have breakthroughs and transformations? Of course. Are there ways that are this much fun, sexy, and beautiful at the same time? I doubt it. Do you have to have a breakthrough? Of course not (although it will probably happen anyway). My theory with our hectic lifestyles—why not multi-task? Look sensual, sexy, feel beautiful, own your power, exercise, and express yourself fully while mesmerizing your man at the same time.

NOW IT'S YOUR TURN

Another opportunity for you to experience The Circle that I mentioned earlier is through some authentic sharing of your own. If you don't have the opportunity to take the actual class to experience The Circle, the following are some suggestions that may give you a taste of what The Circle has to offer. There are 10 questions that will serve as guidelines to get you started on the process of sharing your thoughts. Begin asking yourself and then answering the questions overleaf. You can do this in one of several ways.

1) Answer them with a friend. The key here: DO NOT do this exercise with someone you want approval from. This is very important.

2) If there is not someone you feel safe with, journal your answers. Invest in a beautiful book with blank pages and begin writing down your answers to these

LEAH'S STORY

This is a story of serendipity…if your dance unfolds as life does, it will be an amazing experience.

The Art of Exotic Dancing for Everyday Women™ class started in Philadelphia in 1998 at a business I own called The Learning Studio, which offers classes in everything from cooking, art, yoga, and computers to exotic dancing. One day I had a phone call from a reporter from The Philadelphia Inquirer, *who wanted to write a story about this class and the students. I told her that it was always full and it was much more than sexy dance moves. She took a class so she could write from experience. Her article was entitled "Exercising Your Sex Appeal." She nailed it!*

Then we received calls from two US national TV shows and then women called from all over the country wanting classes or a video. My partner Tim Kelly and I own Philadelphia Films, a film production company, so we created an instructional video based on the class, casting a cross-section of women from the class. Some are profiled in this book.

Next, The Associated Press wrote an article and a subsequent piece by WEB MD was noticed by The Times *in London. Their feature launched the dance class and video in the United Kingdom. We had never even sent out a press release. It was all organic.*

Tim, our instructor Molly, and I were headed to London in May of 2002 to teach our first UK class. Two weeks prior to that, we received an e-mail from Carlton Publishing asking us to author this book. The editor had no idea we were coming to London but as serendipity would have it we met and this book is now in your hands.

The video has gone on to a #1 sales ranking on Amazon.com and the media attention continues. Women everywhere are requesting classes and we are training teachers and offering hundreds of class franchise opportunities. Why? To create space for women… to transform how they feel about their bodies and sensuality, to increase confidence and celebrate their beauty inside and out. The word is spreading like wild fire!

This is an example of life unfolding that applies to the exotic dance experience. Lucky events come our way. If we take action, life and our dance comes together for us. Create a balance between being, seeing, and doing. Don't over-analyze or worry. Let go, move to your inner flow, and you will experience yourself and your life in a whole new way.

questions. The key here: Honesty and authenticity. The more honest and real you are, the bigger the breakthrough.

3) If you have three or more willing girlfriends, create your own Circle and explore these questions among yourself. The key here: No cross talk. We are not fixing anything. We are sharing, listening, and accepting one another.

YOUR BEAUTY BLUEPRINT

This is something every woman possesses and each one has an innate natural pattern. It is what we love about ourselves. Others may appreciate it but we must choose it. You must discover and focus on what makes you a beautiful woman without comparing yourself to others. Your beauty blueprint has both a framework and an inner core; these natural aspects of you are what makes you unique. Think about it now; find your best three characteristics in each category and remember them to boost yourself as you look in the mirror, and throughout your dance.

Framework:		Core features:	
Hair	Hands	Smile	Energy
Skin	Nails	Voice	Thoughts
Face	Breasts	Laugh	Intelligence
Eyes	Butt	Personality	Creativity
Nose	Legs	Humor	Kindness
Mouth	Feet	Talent	Generosity
Teeth	Stomach	Enthusiasm	Openness
Neck	Height	Health	Awareness
Shoulders	Weight	Acceptance	Spirituality
Arms	Other	Spontaneity	Other

WHAT YOU NEED

To learn the moves that make up the routine you will need a full-length mirror, an oversized button down shirt, some sexy heels, and a few songs you love (see the Discography on page 127 for suggestions). Practise your routines in leggings or tights as your basic outfit. And keep an open mind! *So let's get started!*

10 QUESTIONS TO ASK YOURSELF

1 Why did I buy this book and what do I want to learn from it?

2 Do I think I am sensual and sexy? How do I describe sexy?

3 What is my favorite body part?

4 Do I love how I dress, wear my hair, and put on my make-up?

5 How do I feel when I look in the mirror?

6 Do I feel jealous of or competitive with other women?

7 How do I feel when I walk through a room full of people?

8 What would my mother think of exotic dancing?

9 What would my friends think of exotic dancing?

10 What would my partner think about exotic dancing?

Body Language

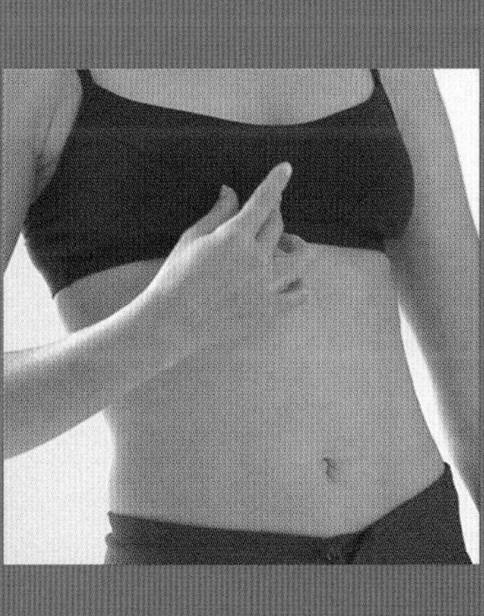

Walking

Walking and eye contact are grouped together here because strong eye contact and good body posture both exhibit confidence and show the world exactly how you feel about yourself. The step-drag walk and strong eye contact establish an air of confidence and can help set the tone for the beginning of your dance.

Remember, nobody walks the same. Be who you are and not like anyone else! Pay attention to your posture and breathing. Walking and eye contact will give you direct access to new levels of confidence. Learn to step-drag walk in bare feet and discover the way your body moves naturally before adding your stripper heels, which can cause you to loose your balance.

As you master the step-drag walk and eye contact, incorporate your heels and accessories.

Walk to the mirror as confidently as possible with no music. Once you feel comfortable with the walking and eye contact, and you feel a level of acceptance about what you are seeing in the mirror, put on the music. As your confidence increases and your sensuality begins to shine through, experiment with all kinds of music (see Discography, *p.127*). This is when it starts to come together. You will be surprised at how your body responds to different music; it can change your mood radically and you will see yourself in lots of new ways. Spend time walking back and forth to the mirror and maintaining a strong eye contact with yourself while listening to different music. It is very important to feel totally relaxed with these moves as they form the springboard on which to frame your dance routine.

WE SAY ...
The basics of walking are the step-drag walk, communication through body language, expression through hand movements, and sending and receiving energy through eye contact. Watch your posture and breathing and focus on your eyes or your partner's.

Walking

1 Begin by standing tall and straight with your shoulders relaxed. Keep your stomach in and your chest out. Then take one step forward toward the mirror. Point your toes to make the walk look more appealing

2 Take the other foot, with the toes pointing downward, and drag the back foot forward and up to meet the heel of the planted foot. Continue moving that foot into a forward step, keeping your toes pointed. Drag the planted foot up and past the other foot. Continue the step-drag walk to the mirror and then walk backward as gracefully as possible.

3 Now add shoes. Exaggerate your hip movements. As your back foot is moving forward, exaggerate the swaying movements up and to the side. Keep your posture straight. Walking backward can be challenging; the important element is to focus on your balance and keep your posture straight. Practise until you feel comfortable moving your body.

Eye Contact

Walk to the mirror confidently, look into your own eyes, and maintain this eye contact with yourself. If you accept the person in the mirror, your partner will too. As you walk to and away from the mirror, focus on what you like about yourself: your eyes, smile, or your walk.

EYE-CONTACT EXERCISES

Clear all the clutter from your mind so that you can be practise these eye-contact exercises with as few distractions as possible. Master eye contact to feel confident in yourself and convey a sensual dance to your partner.

Try Exercise 1

First try solo eye contact. Position yourself in front of the mirror and practise looking into your own eyes. What are they telling you about how you feel inside? Take notice of your inner emotions and how your face and eyes convey what you feel. Practise walking up to the mirror and then away from it. Continue to look into your own eyes and notice what you are feeling about viewing your own reflection. Don't include music yet as it is in the silence that you will hear your own voice. Maintain eye contact with yourself in the mirror, think positive thoughts, and train your inner voice to articulate positive feelings. Keep a positive message or movie rolling in your head to alter your intrinsic energy and project a new positivity to the world.

Smile at yourself in the mirror. Think positive thoughts and banish any negativity—you will soon see your inner beauty.

If you need help to get started, say "I am beautiful, I am sexy," and repeat it over and over until you begin to see and believe it. Find something about yourself that you like. Your hair, skin, eyes, lips, nose, personality. Focus on what you like, not dislike. For most of us, this is a most emotionally challenging exercise. Keep at it, practise, begin to undo all those years of negativity, and re-invent your relationship with yourself. Once you see the beautiful, sexy woman inside, you will develop confidence in yourself that you can share and stop looking for outside approval of your beauty and sex appeal. You can define this for yourself!

Eye Contact

Move on to Exercise 2

Next try dyadic eye contact, which is the art of sending and receiving your energy through eye contact with another person, and is probably the most challenging aspect of exotic dancing. This is how we really connect with our partner on a very intimate level. First pick a partner, preferably someone close to you with whom you feel safe. Try a friend, your lover, or even a trusted work colleague. After choosing a partner, pick a safe, distraction-free environment so you can practise the exercise and focus on your energy.

Try to get your message across through eye contact alone. Look at your partner and think seductive thoughts.

Turn to your partner and decide who will be sending and who will be receiving information. Switch around. To send information, practise saying "hello" with your eyes as you walk toward the receiver, who should be greeting you with their eyes. Do this twice and then reverse positions. Keep at it until it feels comfortable. One or both of you may start laughing or talking—this is natural if you are feeling uncomfortable, but it is important to do this exercise without any verbal communication. Next incorporate your step-drag walk (*see pp.24-25*) and send a seductive message such as "I want you." Notice how you are feeling as you approach your partner. Be clear of your intentions as you project your eye contact. If you are feeling scared, anxious, frustrated, or loving, try to be as clear and open to these emotions as possible. Try to be truly present with your partner. Stand in front of them and attempt to engage their eyes with yours. What are they saying to you? More importantly, what are your own eyes projecting to your partner? Try to look at each other with no pretence or judgments in mind. Block out any negative thoughts that are going on in your head. Pay attention to your body language and posture. Are you giving your partner "mixed intentions" with your eye contact and body language? For example, you may appear open with your eye contact but may be sending mixed signals through your folded arms.

Practise this difficult exercise every day with people that you interact with, socialize with, or work with. Repetition is the key to mastering eye contact. You will find that your ability to communicate improves and also that there is no right or wrong way to project your eye contact.

WE SAY ...

Have you ever wondered why some people can walk into a room full of strangers and command attention while others are hardly noticed? The secret is in the eye contact. What does eye contact say about you? Why do you want to have strong eye contact with others? Number one, it inspires confidence, projects your intentions, connects you with others, and it allows you to take in information about how that person is feeling and what space they are in. So as you walk to the mirror and look at your own eyes, what are you saying to yourself?

We want to be open to receive ourselves. Is this person in the mirror open to what you're doing? Is she happy? Is she feeling comfortable? Does she feel safe? Does she feel safe looking at herself? Does she feel comfortable with what she sees? When you're walking towards the mirror and you're seeing too much cellulite on the thighs and a pot belly where you don't want a pot belly, you need to get past these thoughts because this is the foundation of the whole experiment: What you think is what you feel and what you feel is what you project.

YOU SAY ...

Eileen: *I felt, at first, that I looked like a klutz. The most difficult thing for me in walking was looking at myself, to make eye contact with myself in the mirror. I come from a long history of thinking I'm ugly and so this was a real challenge. I had to do a lot of self-talk, I kept fighting the lies that I've grown up with and keep telling myself, "This is good, this is okay."*

Kecia: *You're trying to be sensual. It's hard enough to look at yourself in the mirror and not criticize the way you look. You're looking at a pimple or bags under your eyes or something. It's hard to say, "You look good today"—this is natural if you are feeling you just have to try to look at the beauty within and take that aspect of it without judging yourself.*

Patti: *I remember after the very first class, I went home and stood in front of the mirror for a good hour. I must've gotten home at like, 11 o'clock, and I was just in the mirror, by myself, and I was dancing and I could see my face turn red, and it was only me in the mirror! All the moves, you have to just keep doing them, you have to keep trying, and practising.*

Basic Transitional Movements

Use these transitional movements to bring your core moves together and form a fluid routine. Introduce them throughout the core moves they relate to. Here you will learn to use hand movements, trace your lines, toss your head, get down to the floor, and to crawl. Only learn these when you feel comfortable with the basic dance movements shown in the previous pages.

USING YOUR HANDS

Your hands are a vital and expressive form of body language so use them to express your feelings to your partner. What are they communicating to him? They should be playing with the energy flowing between you and your partner, bonding you together. Pretend that you can feel this energy, pull it, immerse yourself in it, give it back to your partner, and then pull it back to you. Do this exercise over and over; your hand movements and style of walking will soon begin to reflect this imaginary tie with your partner. Ask him if he'd like to be a part of your dance. Interact with him without touching him. Keep him involved by using eye contact and suggestive body language.

Use your hands to draw your partner's eyes to exactly where you want them. If you like your face, trace your lips or outline your face with your fingers. If you are proud of your stomach, rub your hand sensually and slowly across you stomach and up your side. The same goes for your hips, breasts, or any other body part you wish to draw attention to. Connect with yourself and maintain a steady eye contact with your partner to draw him in to you.

Basic Transitional Movements

TRACING YOUR LINES

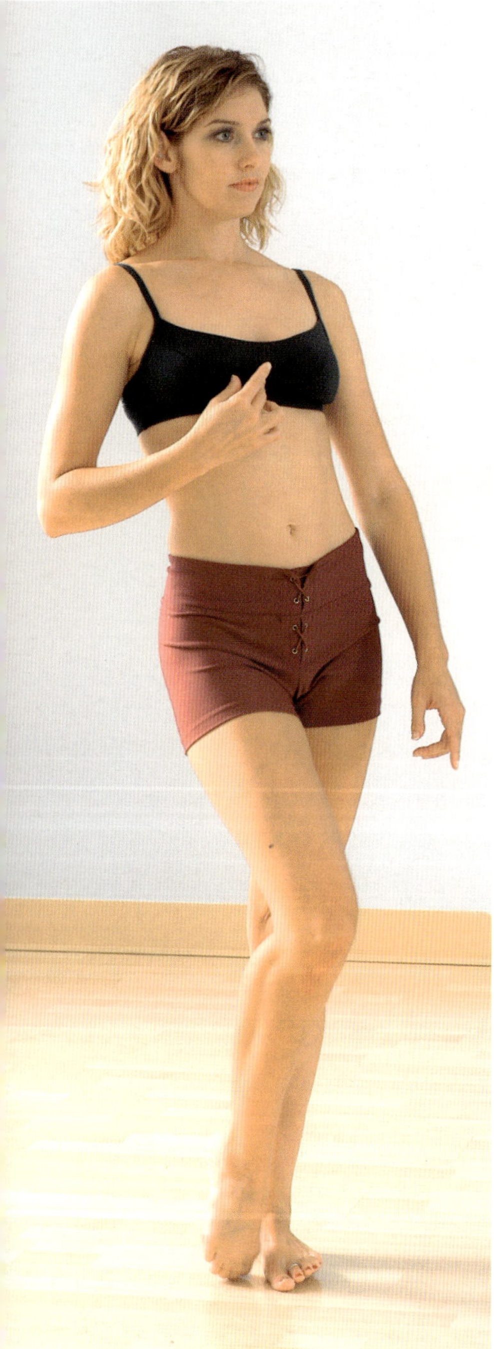

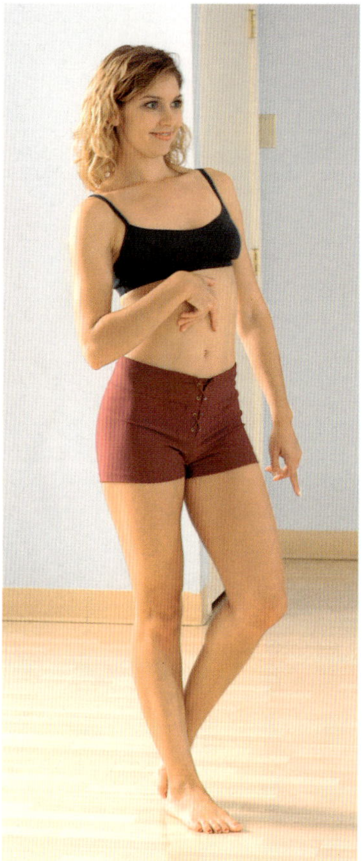

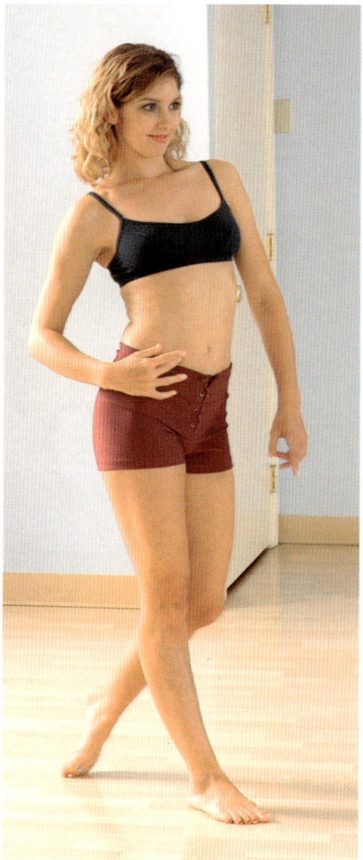

Use this movement to make your dance fluid, flowing, and graceful. Practise tracing the center of your stomach, your face, neck, and the sides of your body with your hands and fingers. If you are feeling very relaxed and comfortable, trace over the top or underneath your breasts. This subtle and suggestive move is much more powerful than simply placing your hand directly on specific areas of your body.

Next trace the lines of inanimate objects, such as the railings of the staircase or the bedpost. By incorporating your hands into a core routine through pushing and pulling energy and tracing your lines, you are well on your way to making your moves look fluid and smooth.

TOSSING HAIR

Incorporate the head toss throughout your dance routine—it is a great transitional move. Roll your neck in a complete circle or flip your head backward and forward, letting your hair fly around you. Pay close attention to the strength of your movement—a slow head toss will appear sensual while a faster one expresses a dominant mood.

WE SAY ...

An effective way to bring your dance together is to combine moves. Here is a combination of tracing your lines with the accentuating move (see p.76) *of gazing at your own body and posing. Although you are dancing, it is fine to slow right down, pose, and then begin to move again. Always remember there is no wrong or right way to do anything. You are free to decide at any time to raise your leg up, strike a pose for a few moments, and then carry on with your dance routine.*

The Striptease

The History of the Striptease

The striptease has its roots in burlesque, which uses comedy to satirize serious matters and has been around for thousands of years. Ancient Greek playwright Aristophanes is known as the "father of burlesque" for his writing. Biblical figure Salome is the first-known striptease dancer.

Burlesque hit the stages of the United States in 1861, with the advent of Lydia Thompson and her Bevy of British Blondes, a troop of exotic dancers. Soon every major city in the US had two or three burlesque theaters featuring female dancers and comic actors. The attraction of the burlesque theaters in the 1930s and early 1940s was that they provided good comic entertainment at an affordable price.

In the meantime exotic dancer Mata Hari debuted on stage at Paris's Musée Guimet in 1905, and soon her erotic act became the talk of the town. With her trademark bejeweled breast cups and flesh-colored body stocking to protect her modesty, she was pivotal in establishing the strip routine as a serious art-form.

The Striptease itself was invented quite by accident years later in 1928 during a burlesque show at Chicago's State Congress Theater. A dancer was changing from an elaborate gown into something skimpier to begin her final dance routine when her lighter garment accidentally fell off. The audience roared with approval and so the Striptease was born. Other famous names associated with the Striptease include Gypsy Rose Lee, who went on to become a Ziegfeld Girl and eventually a serious actress. Sally Rand became notorious for her Lady Godiva stage-act in the 1930s and much later, in the 1960s, Blaze Starr ignited her public with her risqué routines.

Burlesque and the Striptease remained popular into the 1940s until Mayor La Guardia of New York City closed down many of the theaters, accusing their owners of immorality. By then, however, the Striptease was a world-wide phenomenon, enjoyed by millions and destined to live on.

The Striptease has been interpreted by thousands of women down the years—now this is your chance to develop your own routine.

The Hip Rolls—the Stationary Hip Roll

The stationary hip roll is the first in a series of hip rolls. The other three are based on this move. It's a knee-to-waist movement, so keep your ankles still. Not everyone's hips roll in the same direction—some women roll from left to right, others from right to left. Women who can roll their hips both ways are referred to as bi-rollers. Move whichever way feels natural to you.

1 Begin by standing with your feet placed at approximately a shoulder-width apart, with your hands on your hips. Imagine a beam of light passing through the center of your body from your head to the floor, which acts as a pointer on the floor.

2 Pretend that there is a circle on the floor around your feet. Lean slightly backward to engage your stomach muscles and stretch your arms out in front of you, your palms upward, to keep balanced. Bend your knees and keep your hips fluid.

The Way To Win...

by Mike Rothenberger

They tell of the artist who always dreamed of the great works he was going to create. He sat for hours at a time, if anyone would listen, and told of the great paintings he was going to do that would place his name in the halls of fame, there to remain through the indeterminate ages of time. He was going to begin his great work as soon as

him to begin the most important project of his life—but not today. No one ever saw his great paintings, except himself in his own imagination. No one can tell us his name, because no one remembers what it was.

An old proverb says, "The way to do things is to begin." Another reminds us, "Even a journey of a thousand leagues be-

tion, and when we reach it, we will probably find that it is not as difficult as it appeared from the distance. As we approach, it will often diminish as the illusive mirage on the floor of the desert.

It was John Wanamaker who said, "One can walk o'er the highest mountain one step at a time."

imaginary circle and trace the circle on the floor around your feet, tracing the circumference of the circle right through 360 degrees. Place your hands loosely on your hips as you roll them around.

WE SAY ...

It is helpful to put your hands on your hips because that helps you to feel those stomach muscles working. Try drawing big circles and then smaller ones, right down to golf-ball size.

YOU SAY ...

Tammy: *The key is to feel sexy and be relaxed. When I try to look like someone else or execute the move like someone else did it, I think, "Oh, my hips are too big," or "My circle's bigger than hers." But when I just say, "Alright, I'm gonna do this so that it feels sexy," and then it just flows.*

The Revolving Hip Roll

The revolving hip roll is so-called because our bodies turn in the same direction as our hips are already rolling. This move can be quite physically difficult to execute due to the multiple moves combined into one smooth movement. Practise rotating your hips whenever you have a spare moment and eventually the movement will become fluid. Let your instincts lead you.

1 Put your weight on your non-dominant or stationary leg, and move your lead foot out to the edge of your imaginary circle (*see p.38*) and a few inches inward across your body. Raise your heel off the floor and place your hands on your hips.

2 Position your hips directly over your lead foot and then take a small step with this foot around the imaginary circle, crossing it in front of your body. Keep your knees slightly bent and your hands placed loosely on your hips.

3 At the same time, swing your back foot and body around so that you are in the same position as Step One. Practise until your body moves fluidly, and then incorporate your hip roll (*see p.38*). Rotate your body in the same direction as your hips.

WE SAY ...

If you are having trouble with this move, practise on a hardwood floor with socks on or come back to it at a later date when you are feeling more relaxed. Most women get this move when they least expect it.

YOU SAY ...

Molly: *Figure out if you are moving from the left or the right. What comes naturally to your body? When I realized I could move to the right and that was the way my body wanted to go, I practised and practised, and boom, all of a sudden, I learned it and it stuck.*

Bethie: *I went to Hawaii when I was about ten and we were taught hula dancing, so I see this as an extension of hula dancing. When I do it, I'm completely loose. My knees are bent, which gives me the range to play in a circle and I see my hips as drawing circles in the air. Relax and go in circles, and play with it a while.*

The Revolving Hip Roll—Drawing Daisy Petals

There is an exercise designed to help you learn the revolving hip roll (*see pp.40-41*), and this is called "Drawing Daisy Petals on the Floor." Imagine that you form the center of a daisy and the outline of the petals surround you like a circle. Aim to trace the outline of those petals as you revolve around your imaginary circle, rolling your hips all the while.

1 Begin by leaning all your weight on your non-dominant or stationary leg. Keep that knee slightly bent and flexible to allow your other leg to extend forward, with the toes pointed.

2 Keep your back straight as you bend your knee and extend your other foot forward. Trace a daisy petal on the floor around your imaginary circle, with your body remaining at the center of the flower.

3 As you draw one daisy petal on the floor, incorporate your hip roll (*see p.38*) to turn your body to the right. Bend your non-dominant knee again and, keeping your back straight, repeat the movement, extending your leg in front of you and tracing the outline of the flower. Repeat through 360 degrees.

The Squatting Hip Roll

This move will get you a little closer to doing some very sexy work on the floor. It is after learning the squatting hip roll that you will learn the transitional moves to take you down to the floor. Remember the basics: be relaxed, stand within your imaginary circle, and keep your back alternately rounded and arched.

1 Start in the "catcher's position." Keep your feet at a shoulder-width apart and begin by bending forward from your hips. Place your hands loosely above your knees and slowly come down into a squatting position. Keep your arms straight as your hands rest on your knee. Remember to arch your back—straight, long body lines look sexy.

2 When you round your back, your pelvis will naturally move forward. Likewise as you arch your back, your pelvis moves backward naturally. Squat with a rounded back, then move your hips to the left and roll back to the right, and then arch your back. Hold that pose and then return to the rounded back position, holding this pose as well.

3 Imagine a circle on the floor around your feet and a pointer through the center of your body. Pretend to draw circles on the floor by alternately arching and rounding your back while rolling your hips. Experiment by seeing how comfortable you are rolling close to the floor—you will feel this in your thighs. Then roll back into the squatting position.

4 Imagine a circle on the wall behind you and your pointer going through your center. Pretend to draw circles on the wall behind you. Accentuate your rounded and arched back and keep your arms straight to accentuate your long body lines.

YOU SAY ...

Patti: *I didn't feel my back was arched enough, either one way or the other. I could only do so much and as long as I felt comfortable with that, I think I felt comfortable with learning the move.*

Tammy: *I kind of had to stand up and then squat down lots of times, and maybe squat down too far, to see how low I could go down and then find that place in the middle that was the most comfortable.*

The Kneeling Hip Roll

The fourth hip roll in this series is a kneeling hip roll, which is essentially a stationary hip roll (*see p.38*) done on your knees. Use this to move to get from any standing hip roll to the floor. For comfort, kneel on a rug or use a pillow to cushion your knees. This is great to do on a bed!

1 Begin on your knees, keeping a straight back. Spread your knees so that they are a shoulder-width apart. Either balance on your toes or place your feet almost flat on the floor (*see inset*), depending on which is more comfortable for you.

2 Imagine you have a beam of light going through your center and pointing at the floor below you, then draw a circle on the floor by rolling your hips around. Trace big circles or little circles, letting your stomach muscles do their job.

3 This pose looks very sexy if you lean back further on your heels. To really spice up this move, grab your heels as you lean back and do the hip roll. As you become more flexible, you will be able to roll back all the way onto your back and roll up again.

WE SAY ...

*Practise these moves with your eyes closed so you can feel the mechanics of exactly which body part is interacting with which. Raise your hands above your head or run your fingers through your hair. Other options are to hold onto the back of your head (*see left*) or rest your hands on your stomach in the hook and grab (*see p.77*).*

If you have bad knees, try this move with your knees together or skip it completely, just coming down to a sitting position. Don't hurt yourself or cause discomfort. There's no wrong way to do these poses.

YOU SAY ...

Anne Marie: *A challenging part of the kneeling hip roll is getting down to your knees gracefully. I find that if I take it very slowly, don't rush it, just move smoothly, that it's not as difficult as it looks. Also, use a prop, maybe a chair, or just lean against the door jamb and move slowly.*

Kecia: *If you have a problem with your knees, do the movement on the soft part of your knees instead of on the front part of them. Or use a pillow or make sure you have a carpet or something for support.*

More Transitional Movements

GETTING DOWN ON THE FLOOR

There are several ways to get down to the floor. One is to lower yourself without using any props. If you want to use props such as a mirror, door jamb, bedpost, wall, or even your partner, these are covered in the section on props (*see pp.78-91*).

To reach the floor without using a prop, put one foot out in front of you and let your hand guide you down to the floor. Put one knee down, then the other, and begin the kneeling hip roll (*see p.46*).

After completing the kneeling hip roll, you may want to get down to the floor to begin your floorwork routine (*see pp.52-57*). Put your hands flat on the floor in front of you for support and then simply sit down on your butt or your hip. There you go—you're on the floor. Do this slowly and it looks very sexy.

More Transitional Movements

USING THE CRAWL

Use the crawl to get into position for floorwork (*see pp.52-57*), after pushing off a prop, to move from the kneeling hip roll (*see p.46*) to floorwork, or to get into a sitting position at the end of your routine. Move forward, crawling along the floor, accentuating the dip in your back. Stretch your body languidly as you move from place to place.

GETTING UP FROM THE FLOOR

End your routine on the floor in a pose, or be more dominant by getting back to standing. Bend one leg and place that foot flat on the ground. Put your weight on this leg and move the other leg forward so that you are squatting in an animal-like pose. Slink up to standing, turn, begin to walk away, and strike a pose looking back over your shoulder.

The Floorwork Routine

Floorwork is essentially a series of poses connected by transitional moves, and is usually considered to be the most sensual part of the art of exotic dancing. Most importantly, it can put both you and your partner in the mood for the final act, the Striptease (*see pp.64-71*). Take a deep breath and relax. Figure out which movements feel right to you and learn to make the connections between them gracefully; then try to develop some poses of your very own.

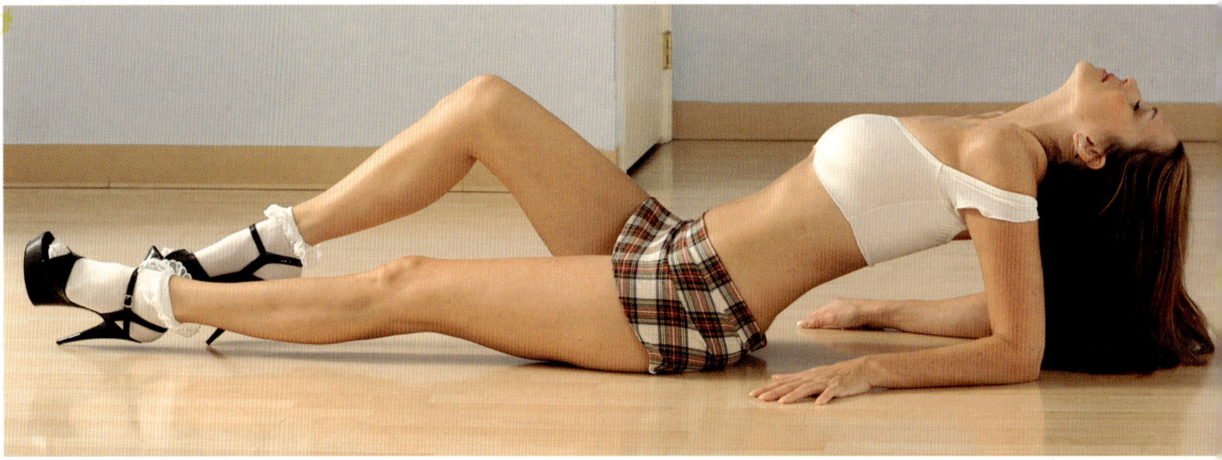

1 Stretch out on the floor and lean back on your elbows, with your palms flat on the floor. Stretch your legs out and bend one knee upward. Arch your back, let your head hang loosely back, and then strike a pose.

2 With palms still on the floor, bend both your knees (*see inset*), cross your ankles, and draw your knees to your chest.

3 Draw your feet straight up and draw a few circles in the air with your toes (*see inset*), keeping your legs slightly bent and flexible at the knees. Try to keep your head tilting backward and your lower arms flat against the floor for support.

4 Now try the "cricket pose," and rub your shins together, brushing your feet up and down. Cross your legs slightly over each other, tighten your abdominal muscles, and slowly lower your legs to the floor. Let your head hang back, linger in the moment, stretch, pose, and take a breath.

The Floorwork Routine

5 From lying down, raise your head, bring your right foot up next to your left knee, and turn onto your left side.

6 Now trace your lines (*see p.32*). Follow the outline of your body from top to bottom and then back up to the top.

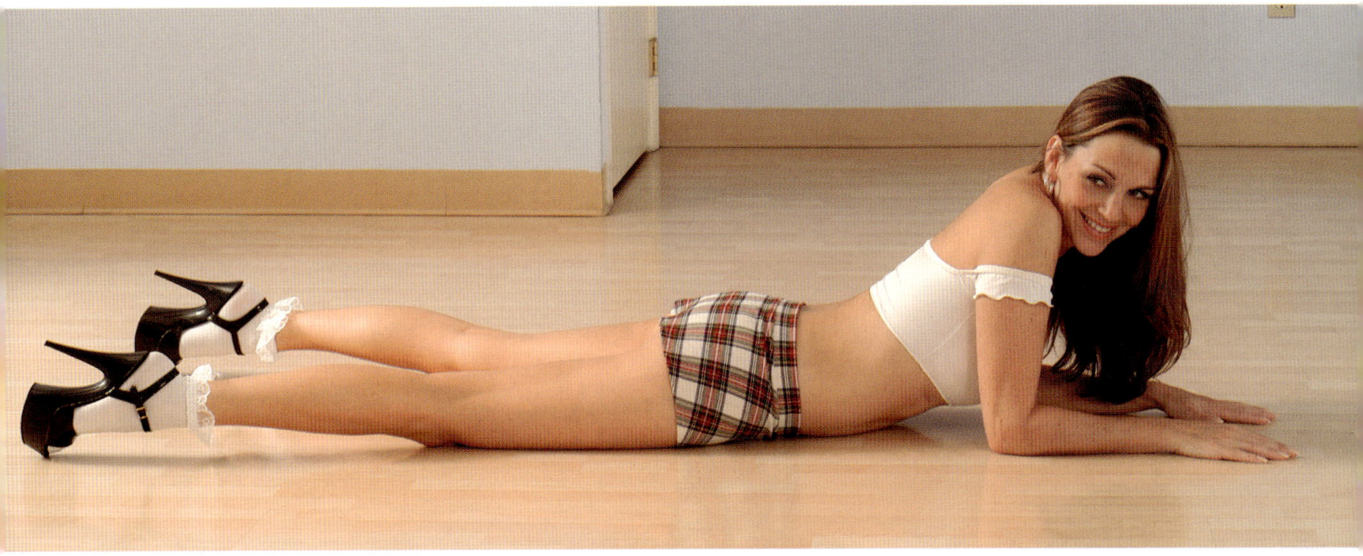

7 Turn over onto your stomach, keeping your body lines long and straight. Point your toes toward the floor and support yourself on your forearms. Look longingly at your partner.

8 Push yourself up onto your knees for the "rock'n'roll" hip roll. With your arms outstretched, slope your back. Trace a circle on the wall with your hips and remember to alternately round and arch your back in the squatting hip roll (*see p.44*).

The Floorwork Routine

9 From the squatting position, roll back down onto your stomach. From there roll over onto your left side once more and bend your right knee forward over your left knee (*see Step 5*), with the right toes tucked behind the left knee.

10 Depending on your flexibility, either raise your right leg straight up into the air or halfway up, keeping it bent at the knee. Support your leg with your right arm. Both these moves look very sexy when performed slowly.

11 Bring your right leg slowly down to the floor, turn over onto your bottom, sit up, and end with a nice, arched stretch and pose.

WE SAY ...

*Take your time and linger in the moment of these poses—be tender with yourself. When developing poses of your own, remember that anything you feel comfortable with can count as a pose. Any move can be a part of your floorwork routine and you can make anything look sexy. Slow stretching can be incredibly sexy if you do it with purpose and good posture. There are at least three ways to get down to the floor. Use a prop, try a modified move, using your hands to guide you to the floor, or slide from the kneeling hip roll (*see p.46*) directly to a sitting position.*

YOU SAY ...

Bethie: *Floor work was uncomfortable. It was uncomfortable because, I don't know, that's where my hurdle thing comes in, my whole reason for taking the class. And I'm like, "Uh oh, this is like, mega-acting sexy now and I am not ready for this." So it was really hard for me. I put myself in a field and it helped a lot. Mentally I'm in a field doing these moves. If you can take yourself away mentally, you'll be amazed at what hurdles you can get over. If you have any special limitations, you can modify any move, or choose not to do it, or do something else totally different. It's up to you.*

Advanced Floorwork Moves

Here are some more strenuous moves that can be added to your floorwork routine as you become more flexible and strong. Only try these exercises when you feel ready for them.

1 As you come out of the "rock'n'roll" hip roll (*see p.55*) and onto your left side, extend your right leg straight up at right angles to your body. Bend your left arm to support your weight and grasp your right leg with your right arm.

2 Slowly bring your leg back down to the floor, supporting yourself with your elbow. Sit up and stretch out your legs at more than a shoulder-width apart.

3 Bend slowly forward, keeping a straight back, and grasp your legs as close to the ankles as you can. Maintain eye contact with your partner and create a sensual pose with your breast and neckline while you bend forward.

Advanced Floorwork Moves

4 Bend one knee and bring that foot in toward your body, stretching the other leg up in the air and out to the side of your body. Keep a light hold on your ankles. Repeat this movement with the other leg.

5 Lift both legs slowly into the air to form a "V" shape, still clasping your ankles. Keep your body weight forward so you do not fall backward.

6 Lower your legs and complete your routine with a stretch and pose. Keep your arms and legs straight and your lines long. Arch your back.

Visualization

In order to feel relaxed and calm to dance for your partner, you need to be in a safe and happy mindset. Learn these easy visualization techniques to remove the chaos of outer life from your mind. Read the following visualization a few times, close your eyes, relax, and escape. If you have the means, read this visualization into a recorder in a soft, soothing voice with some calming music in the background. Then you can play it back and use it for yourself.

Lie down wherever you feel comfortable, whether on a bed or a mat on the floor. Take a nice, deep breath in and imagine the sun shining down on your skin. It is warm and creates a feeling of relaxation deep within you. Touch your arm ever so gently and feel the warmth on your skin. Smell the scent of the most beautiful flowers you've ever seen. Take a deep breath in. As you look across this beautiful field of flowers, notice that they are every color you can imagine. Breathing in, you feel warm, relaxed, and notice a butterfly or two. You feel relaxed and alive in all this color. You hear birds in the distance. Breathe it all in, taking in everything around you. Run your hand across the ground and become aware of the blades of grass tickling the palm of your hand. Take your finger and run it up your own arm, gently and softly. Be tender with yourself. The breeze runs through your hair and across your cheeks, carrying the scent of these beautiful flowers. Touch your face gently and run your fingers through your hair. The sun, warm on your skin, feels safe and comfortable. Think about this, or any other place that makes you feel calm and peaceful. Remember how it feels. Now come back to the room you're in, open your eyes, and look around you. Carry that feeling of peace with you inside your own body and stay relaxed and centered in all these floorwork poses.

Allow yourself to relax completely and drift off, formulating some of your own relaxing thoughts and images. Try putting on soft, comforting music to soothe away your cares, or record a visualization to replay when you want to relax.

The Striptease

It is time to introduce you to the Striptease. This is simply all the moves that you've learned so far but incorporating a shirt. So grab a shirt and get ready to perform. Use a large button-down shirt—a man's shirt works great and many men find that very sexy. Smooth materials like silk work best although you should use whatever makes you feel sexy.

1 Button the shirt's bottom button. This will enable you to slip the shirt gracefully from your shoulders and drop it to the floor later in the routine. Sway your hips back and forth and open and close your shirt, keeping eye contact with your partner.

2 When you have your partner's full attention, cross your arms in front of you and slide your right hand under the left shoulder of your shirt, pushing it slowly off your shoulder. Maintain eye contact all along.

3 Slide your left hand effortlessly from inside the sleeve and allow the shirt to drop slowly off your left shoulder. Hold the shirt with your right hand and slide your left hand from the sleeve. Trace your lines and keep communicating with your partner.

4 Hold your shirt at waist height and begin to play with it. Trace your lines and sway your hips gently from side to side, stepping forward and backward. Twirl the shirt sleeve as if it was a feather boa (*see p.90*).

5 Drop the shirt and perform a quarter-revolving hip roll (*see p.40*) or simply gently step to the side. After turning, try a squatting hip roll (*see p.44*) and turn the shirt around as you come back up so that the buttons are facing the back.

6 Turn back towards your partner, raise your shirt up to cover the front of your body, and gently take it in your mouth. Continue moving slowly from side to side and make sure you maintain a strong and flirty eye contact with your partner during this move.

7 With the shirt still in your mouth, slowly take each bra strap down. Keep moving from side to side or backward and forward as you pull each strap down, and keep a strong eye contact going with your partner all the time.

8 With the shirt still in your mouth, slowly unhook your bra with one hand. A front-closure bra come in handy at this stage—although you can unhook your bra at the back, a front-fastener is much less fiddly.

The Striptease

9 Still holding your shirt in front of your body, use your other hand to slide your bra from underneath your shirt. Show it to your partner and lasso it above your head. Continue to move seductively as you play with your bra.

10 Drop your bra on the floor and lower your shirt until it just covers your breasts. Roll them gently underneath your shirt. Pose for several moments as you do this, all the while looking directly into your partner's eyes.

11 Still maintaining that eye contact, slowly and provocatively bend over toward your partner. Lower the shirt slightly to reveal a little more of your breasts to him, but do not remove the shirt altogether—make him wait.

12 Slowly stand upright again, cross your arms in front of you, and either perform a revolving hip roll (*see p.44*) or simply turn around. Sway your hips from side to side and then pose for a few lingering moments.

13 Start to walk away, letting the shirt fall to the ground as you move. Cover your breasts with your hands, strike a pose, and look back at your partner with your most seductive eye contact.

WE SAY ...

We urge you to practise the moves over and over until they become comfortable. Once you feel comfortable with them, you can incorporate a step-drag walk (see p.24)*. Keep eye contact with your partner and practise improving your balance and body posture. Sway your hips back and forth, open and close your shirt. Keep your body in continual motion as you slowly undress.*

If you are uncomfortable dropping your shirt completely at the end of the striptease, keep the shirt around your waist as you move into a floorwork routine (see pp.52-57)*. This gives you greater coverage for longer and you can crawl out of your shirt when you want.*

Remember that you never have to do this dance for anyone. If you feel comfortable and safe with your partner, it certainly can be a wonderful, playful, spicy addition to your relationship. If you are not comfortable, or if you do not have anyone to dance for, regard the dance as an expression of yourself.

YOU SAY ...

Molly: *Striptease is anything you want it to be. You can keep yourself as covered as you want. You can take off everything; you can take it off as you're walking; you can really make that your own thing.*

Patti: *Do as much or as little as you want. It's okay to be uncomfortable and it's also okay to feel comfortable with it.*

Ann Marie: *It was an opportunity for me to step out of my comfort zone and to express myself through music and dance, which was very freeing. Once you learn the moves, the music is playing, and you begin to feel more comfortable, it releases a lot of inhibitions.*

Eileen: *I will say "strut your stuff." I want to say, "Walk tall, walk proud."*

Carolyn: *The visual presentation that you're making is one of flowering sensuality—and flowers don't need all their petals open to look incredibly beautiful.*

Tammy: *I've always felt very strongly, very passionately, about my sexuality but have never had a safe way to express it. This is it.*

Molly: *You really can do it. Everyone can do it. It's all in your attitude. Use a mirror so you can see yourself. Get a big shirt and a pair of sexy heels, and get ready for the ride.*

Putting it all Together—the Complete Routine

Step-Drag Walk, page 24.

Stationary Hip Roll, page 38.

Squatting Hip Roll, page 44.

Mirror Sliding, page 86.

Mirror Sliding, page 86.

Kneeling Hip Roll, page 46.

Practise your dance moves and then put them all together, incorporating the core routines, transitional movements, and accentuating movements. Bring your confidence; put on sexy heels and play music that moves you.

1 Walk toward your mirror or whatever prop you have at home, using the step-drag walk and keeping eye contact with yourself. Step backward and then step-drag walk back toward the mirror, utilizing the hook-and-grab accentuating movement.

2 Stop about a foot away from the mirror or chosen prop. Place your legs at a shoulder-width apart, do a few stationary hip rolls, and then transfer your whole body weight onto your stationary or non-dominant leg. Do the revolving hip roll. Turn completely around once and continue moving until you are side-on to the mirror or your body is at right angles to your prop.

3 Bend from your hips and do a number of squatting hip rolls. Draw imaginary circles on the floor below you and on the wall behind you.

4 Slink up to standing. Pivot on one foot and step-drag walk gracefully away from the mirror.

5 Do the revolving hip roll to turn and face the mirror and step-drag walk forward.

6 About one foot away from your mirror or prop, stop, lean in, and place both hands above your head in a "spread-em" pose on the prop. Step in closer, raise one hand up higher, and turn toward this arm. Carry on turning until you can lean your back against the prop, all the time keeping your arms raised at different heights. Turn around.

7 While leaning against the prop, do a few "chorus-line" kicks by making big circles in the air with either foot.

8 Place one foot behind the other and slide elegantly down or do a hip roll to the floor.

9 Once you are down on the floor, push off gently from the prop with one hand and crawl away. Perform a few kneeling hip rolls before beginning your floorwork routine (*see pp.52-59*). Grab the back of your shoes and do more kneeling hip rolls. Sit back between your feet, and, if you are supple enough, lay back full-length on the floor.

10 Come back to a sitting position and move over onto your side with your legs bent to the side of your body. Slowly explore your body as though it was the first time you have ever felt it.

11 Continue with the entire floorwork routine. End up on the floor or come up to standing again and move straight on to your Striptease routine, using an oversized shirt (*see pp.64-71*).

Revolving Hip Roll, page 40.

Putting it all Together—the Complete Routine

You have been given the basics for a series of sexy and intriguing sequences and moves. It is now up to you to decide how to put them together; what feels good for you? Spend time practising and get to know your body. You will soon learn to move fluidly between positions.

ACCENTUATING MOVES

Striking a Pose
This is good to do when you are moving in between moves or if you want to accentuate a certain movement. Linger in a languid pose for a few seconds before slowly and fluidly moving on to your next position.

Stretching Your Lines
To show off your body to its full extent, stretch slowly while executing your sequences of moves. The long, lean lines will draw attention to the shapes and curves of your body as you move from pose to pose.

Gazing at Your Body
Look at yourself with love and admiration; this allows you to draw attention to the area of your body you want to show off—your observer will automatically look where you are looking. Use this along with tracing your lines.

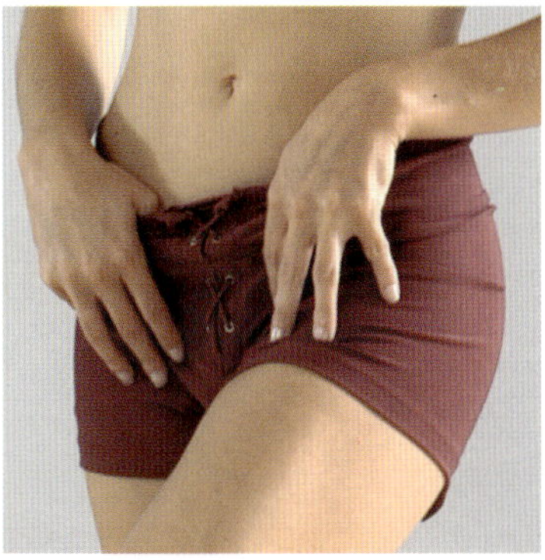

Hooking and Grabbing

Hook your thumbs under the waist of your pants and then grab some of the fabric. This presents a picture in which you look like you are ready to pull your pants down to reveal what is hidden beneath. This is effective when done with the step-drag walk (*see p.24*) or the hip rolls (*see pp.38-47*).

Slinking from Move to Move

Try this method to move from a squatting position with your body bent forward to a fully upright position. Round your shoulders forward and let your arms fall loosely, with the palms facing outward. Round your back up to a straight position and slowly drag your palms along the inside of your thighs to the front of your abdomen and then upward to your waist. Complete the movement by pushing your shoulders upward and continuing until standing up straight.

Playing Slowly with Your Hair

Running your fingers through your hair is a very sensual move and gives you something to do with your hands.

USING A BEDPOST

If you are dancing in the bedroom you can incorporate a bedpost into your routine. It is a great alternative if you do not have a pole at home. You can do a hip-roll down the post, tracing your imaginary circle as you slide down, or execute a simple slide. If your bedpost is high, keep your hands above your head. If it is a lower bedpost, use your hands to stabilize yourself against the post as you slowly slide downward. Always remember to maintain a strong eye contact with your partner.

WE SAY ...

Bedposts are fun to incorporate into your dance routine to add variety. The trick here is to place your hands on the bedpost to stabilize yourself as you slide downward, but remember—try not to look as though you are hanging onto it for dear life. This will just make your whole routine look really clumsy! For variation in your routine, play with other items found around the house. We have made some more suggestions on the following pages. Remember never to do anything that makes you feel uncomfortable.

Using Props at Home

THE STAIRS

Crawling up the Stairs

Slowly lean up the stairs, with your knees and hands each on four different consecutive steps. Stretch your body out, arch your back, and keep your toes pointed. Depending if you are crawling to or away from your partner, look back or up ahead and maintain a strong, seductive eye contact. Start crawling slowly upward, step by step.

Doing a Hip Roll

Position yourself facing forward on the stairs, with your hands and feet approximately two steps apart. With straight arms and an arched back, use your arms to lift yourself away the stairs. Do a hip roll (*see p.38*) with your internal pointer either facing down at the step beneath you or toward the wall in front of you. Use leg kicks combined with the hip rolls to enhance your routine on the stairs.

Using Props at Home

The banister is another prop to incorporate into your dance on the stairs. Strike a pose and use the banister to accentuate or frame your body line. Keep your posture long and your eye contact a seductive "come play with me" type of look.

You can incorporate the walk by coming down the stairs toward your partner or enticing them up the stairs with your walking, eye contact, and posing. As with most of these moves, good eye contact with your partner creates the strong connection you are looking for.

WARNING ... Remember to be careful when you go through your routine on the stairs—it is easy to twist an ankle.

SLIDING DOWN A MIRROR

1 Take a step toward the mirror and stand about eight inches away to leave yourself enough room for turning around. Place your hands gently against the mirror at different heights, step slightly back on one foot, and lean slowly and seductively in toward the mirror, looking down at your reflection.

2 Push back slightly and slowly turn yourself around by pivoting on your front foot. Take half a step forward with your back foot and lean gently back toward the mirror. Leave one hand raised and draped against the mirror and perform a lengthy standing stretch (*see p.78*) as you turn around.

3 To slide down the mirror, position your feet a shoulder-width apart. Use the mirror to keep your balance and begin to slide gently down. Either slide straight down the mirrror, bending your knees to the floor, or incorporate a stationary hip roll (*see inset*) into your movement.

4 As you slide, push yourself gently away from the mirror until you are kneeling on the floor, with your knees a shoulder-width apart. Keeping one hand raised and brushing the mirror, lean your head backward and arch your back to get into position for the kneeling hip roll (*see p.46*).

Accessories

Once you feel confident with your moves and routines, start to experiment a little. Utilize household items to introduce some fun and spontaneity into your movements; play with a towel or add a feather boa to your outfit. A long, pretty scarf or shawl will work just as well.

PLAYING WITH A TOWEL

1 Wrap yourself in a large, soft towel and expose the left side of your body slightly. Turn around and slowly move the towel across your body from left to right to expose your right side as you turn.

2 Cover your body with the towel. Turn your back on your partner and let the towel slip down to your butt. Raise it, cross it in front of you, and repeat so that the towel rises and falls again.

WE SAY ...

Use a towel as a fun and impromptu move. Do it before you get in the shower or when you get out—whenever your partner is not expecting it. Practise ahead of time so that your movements look smooth and fluid, and pay attention to your posture. Alternate between gazing at your own body and looking seductively at your partner.

3 Swing round, grasp the towel with both hands, and pull it up in front of you so it falls down your body. Expose your left leg, bend it slightly, and balance on your toes. Linger in that position.

4 Raise your left leg and use your heel to push the towel between your legs. Catch it with your left hand and pull it backward and forward, tucking your left foot behind your right knee.

USE A FEATHER BOA

1 Combine the sensuality of dance with the fun of a feather boa, using it to help conceal certain body areas as you move. Create a sense of mystery to tempt your audience by alternately crossing and uncrossing the boa in front of you.

2 Use the boa to trace your body lines (*see inset*) from side to side and playfully run it up and down your body behind you.

3 Incorporate your feather boa into a kneeling hip roll (*see p.46*) by combining it with the hand movements you usually make during your routine. Brush the boa slinkily up and down your body and gently around your legs (*see inset*).

4 Lie back, stretch out, bend one leg, and arch your back. Let the feathers gently fall across your face. Hold that pose for several moments.

Getting Fit

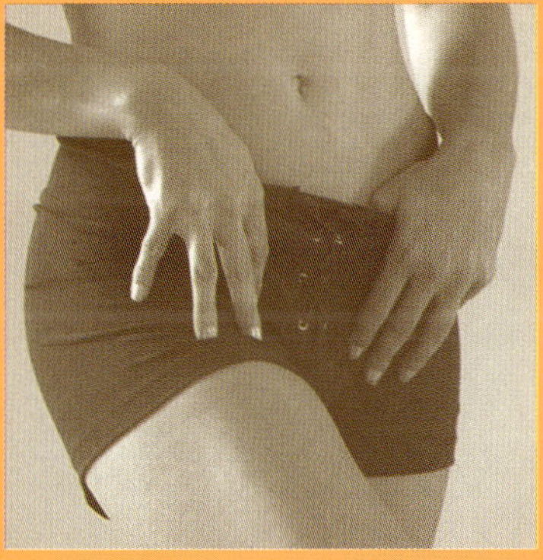  

Health and Fitness

The Art of Exotic Dancing for Everyday Women™ is a fun, sexy workout for women of all ages. It is a workout for your body, mind, and soul. With the help of some great music, you can dance your way to health and fitness. Unlike other workouts, exotic dancing is fun, it expands you as a woman, and leaves you feeling sensual, which is great for your mental health as well.

Women of all ages, shapes, and sizes will gain tremendous benefits from exotic dancing. Young and fit as well as the overweight and over-40s can do this. It is easy because you can do the routine to the degree that works for you. Roll down a little bit or go all the way to the floor, whatever you can manage. The important part is to get your body moving to the music; then you won't even realize what a great workout you are getting.

A balanced diet will help you feel good about yourself and keep your body in good shape, but do remember a healthy mind is just as important.

The best forms of exercise are the ones where you are focused on the activity and you do not even notice you are working out. Sports are like that and so is dancing. With dancing, if you focus on the music and your movements, you forget that you are doing something wonderful for your health. Exotic dancing gives a great work out to your sensuality, self-expression, confidence, and inhibitions as well as your muscles.

FEEL THE BENEFITS OF THE WORKOUT

The Art of Exotic Dancing for Everyday Women™ and StripFit™ are fantastic ways to work out body and soul and to exercise your sex appeal. Walking and making eye contact will connect your mind, body, and spirit. Once that simple connection is made, the exercises will strengthen and tone your body.

Stationary hip rolls loosen the hip flexors and are great exercise for the waistline. The revolving hip roll combines grace and balance and gives your bum and legs, specifically your calves, a great workout. Squatting hip rolls are great for your stomach and thighs. If you push yourself, revolving closer to the floor heightens the effect. Kneeling hip rolls keep your tummy flat, and if you roll back with your

hands on your heels you will achieve the maximum results. Floorwork is excellent to stretch and tone muscles. You will see similar results with yoga or Pilates as they also elongate the muscles. Walking in your heels will give you killer calves so I suggest walking around the house in them as often as possible. This will also give you great practice and have you dancing in heels like a pro. With repetition, these moves will have you toned and fit in no time.

WALK IN HEELS

When you select your heels pay particular attention to how they fit. Be sure they are not too tight or pinching your feet otherwise you will cause corns and blisters. Do not buy shoes that are loose or you may lose your balance and hurt yourself. No matter how pretty a pair of shoes look, be sure they fit. You will be so much more comfortable during your dance.

TAKE CARE OF YOUR BODY

Before beginning any exercise program it is important to consult a physician. If you have any health issues whatsoever, such as a bad back, knees, joint problems, high blood pressure, or you are pregnant, always consult your physician first. Once you obtain approval from your doctor, you may need to modify your moves.

Begin by using slow music so your body moves slowly. Don't exaggerate your hip movements. Incorporate more posing into your dance and avoid the squatting and kneeling hip rolls. There is plenty you can do with walking, posing, the stationary hip roll, and minimal floorwork on your back. To get to the floor, come straight down slowly. Then get up slowly and walk back and forth before launching into the Striptease out of an oversized shirt to complete your routine. Remember, anything can be part of your dance. There is no right or wrong way.

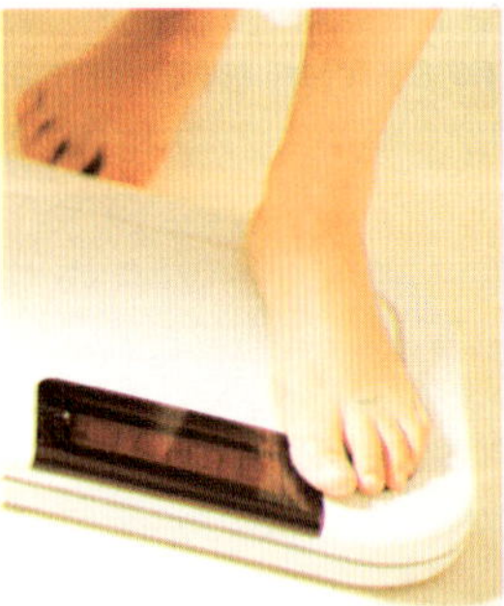

Don't worry about your weight or level of fitness; just do the exercise you feel capable of.

Exotic dancing is also great for any woman with health problems. Ten percent of the women who auditioned to be in the instructional video were breast cancer survivors. They said it helped them re-connect to their femininity and the creative self that gets killed off along with the chemotherapy. I have seen women with health problems come back to life before my eyes.

ANNE MARIE'S STORY

Why would a 54-year-old sales manager take an exotic dance class? Anne Marie wanted to try something she had never done before. It was an opportunity for her to expand her comfort zone. "I met some great people and had a great experience." This was an opportunity to learn how to be more comfortable with herself and to express herself through the dance, which is very liberating. When making the exotic dancing video, Anne Marie was having chemotherapy and radiation therapy for breast cancer. Looking forward to the classes and her bond with other women brought her through this tough time in her life. "Dancing, laughing, and feeling good about ourselves is the best possible medicine."

Eat well, exercise, and above all, let your sense of humor come to the forefront when you are practising your dance. It is meant to be fun!

CLEAR YOUR MIND

Practise exotic dancing on a regular basis to make the connection between your mind, body, and spirit. Subconscious attitudes and outlooks contribute significantly to overall health so your attitude and outlook toward yourself is guaranteed to improve, which has to be beneficial for your health.

Expressing yourself authentically is good for the soul. By facing yourself in the mirror during walking and eye contact, and taking responsibility for negative thoughts, you can create a clearing and give yourself the space to re-invent your relationship with yourself. It is in this clearing that you'll rediscover or create your most sensuous self. Exotic dancing is a great boost to mental health. If you feel sluggish or depressed, put on some music and get dancing to release endorphins and give yourself an energy boost. You will soon find yourself laughing and having fun. It is important for the mind and body connection that your mental health is at peak performance, so put on your dancing shoes and get moving!

StripFit™

Get fit and sexy at the same time! StripFit™ is a one-hour fitness routine based on the core exotic dance moves in previous sections. It was designed for busy women who want to be in great shape and increase their sexual prowess. The core StripFit™ moves will get you started.

1 **Crosswalk with Hook and Grab**. This move combines walking with the accentuating move of the hook and grab (*see p.75*). Take several steps forward. Throw your hips from side to side and hook the thumb of your hands into the top of your pants while walking to and from the mirror.

2 **Pose with Butt Tap**. Combines walking and eye contact (*see p.23*). Strike a pose with one hip pushed out and do a static stretch with the length of your body. Place your hand on your behind and gaze over your shoulder. Give your behind a nice love tap. Continue walking up and back to the mirror.

WE SAY ...

Exercising your sex appeal with some lively music is a great way to get fit and sensual all at the same time. The ten moves shown above will start you off; they are all designed with fitness and sensuality in mind. Being healthy and fit is vital for your well-being and makes you feel better about yourself and thus more confident; the better you feel in yourself, the more expressive, beautiful and sexy you are.

3 **The Corkscrew**. Utilizes the squatting hip roll (*see p.44*). A butt blaster! Your thigh muscles burn as you combine the elements of the squatting hip roll to perform this move. As you lower yourself into a catcher's position, slowly rotate and twist your hips around in a direction that feels comfortable.

4 **Hamstring Stretch**. Makes use of tracing your lines (*see p.32*). Position your feet at two o'clock, arch your lower back, and slide your hands down one leg. As you reach towards your toes, trace your lines. To work on your calf muscles, point your toes and slide down, tracing your lines as you bend.

5 **Pelvic Thrust**. Yoga enthusiasts will love this sexy move! Sit on the floor with your feet flat on the ground and knees at 45 degrees. At first, place both hands behind you for balance. Later rest on one arm. Raise your pelvis towards the ceiling and then lower it again. Your thighs should be parallel with the floor.

6 **Plan K**. Raise your pelvis toward the ceiling and extend one leg, pointing the toes on that foot. Repeat, lower yourself, and switch legs. This gives defined triceps and deltoids.

7 **Hamstring Stretch.** Stretching is sensual. Pick a comfortable position on the floor and extend your legs out, forming a "V." Flex your feet toward the ceiling and stretch toward your foot. As you stretch, trace your lines and gaze at your hands. This move stretches hamstrings and gives your legs a long, lean look.

8 **Scissors.** Sit on the floor, lean back, and place both forearms on the floor. As in floorwork (*see pp.52-57*), raise your legs as high as you can and scissor them, crossing at the ankles. Repeat this to work inner thighs and abdominal muscles.

9 **Side Crunch**. While in the kneeling position, lean to one side and place the palm of your hand on the ground. Place your other hand behind your head. Lift your outside leg up into the air, creating the feeling of squeezing the muscles at your waist. This works out your abdominals, triceps, and hip flexors.

10 **Child's Pose**. Cool down with this variation of the yoga world's child's pose. Begin by kneeling and placing the tops of your feet on the floor. Tuck your buttocks over your feet and stretch your arms straight out on the floor as far as you can in front of you. Relax your entire body into this pose and breathe deeply. Hold the pose until you can feel all the tension draining away.

WE SAY ...

StripFit™ is a one-hour fitness workout based on the core moves of The Art of Exotic Dancing for Everyday Women™, *as shown on pages 64-70. Designed to get you fit and sexy, the full workout will have you looking your best in a few weeks. The abbreviated workout utilized here will start you on your way to being toned and feeling sexy. It is great practice for exotic dancing while getting fit. Being fit is not critical to feeling sexy but it does help you to feel better about yourself. The complete workout video, as well as the* StripFit™ Bums & Thighs *and* StripFit™ Abs, *is available at* artofexoticdancing.com.

Age is Irrelevant

One of the extraordinary things about the Art of Exotic Dancing for Everyday Women™ classes and videos is the women who respond to them. It is not just young girls who attend but women of all ages, shapes, and sizes, who have one very important thing in common: they all know deep within that they are still beautiful and sensual human beings.

As women age, they sometimes feel pressurized to dress and act a certain way. If we believe what we see in magazines, on television, and in the movies, sensuality and beauty appear to be reserved solely for youth. Well, this just isn't so. Women in their 50s, 60s, and 70s can rediscover (or even discover for the first time in some cases) the hidden woman inside: the one who felt beautiful and sensual at her prom, or on her wedding day, at a holiday party, on vacation.

Learning the art of exotic dancing (AOED) can transport you back to that time, place, and special feeling as well as give you new tools to access them anytime, anywhere, at your convenience. It is an empowering experience to let go of your inhibitions and reconnect with your inner self at an age when other people are telling you to slow down! Many women also look forward to the classes as a way to bond with new friends, who can be a huge support when life gets tough. Dancing, laughing, and feeling good about yourself is the best medicine!

CHOOSE AN OUTFIT FOR YOUR DANCE

What to wear if you are slightly older? You may get a buzz out of dressing up as a schoolgirl or a dominatrix, but if you feel that you have grown out of the ideas in fashion on pages 118-121, the best idea is to go with the classic romantic look of silky, sexy, lingerie or a feminine dress, accompanied by soft music.

The music that you find romantic is very personal—it could be anything from Frank Sinatra to Luther Vandross. See page 127 for suggestions. Candles, rose petals strewn around the room, and sensuous scents all go toward creating an great atmosphere in which to perform your dance. **Mindset**: love and romance.

When performing your dance, choose an outfit that you are comfortable with. You can feel and look gorgeous without exposing too much flesh!

Age is Irrelevant

WE SAY ...

The reasons for taking the AOED class vary for each woman, but there is an obvious consistent transformation that takes place in the lives of those who have a hard time seeing their own beauty. Women of all ages, shapes, and sizes echo these sentiments. They are able to address the issues and the changes in their bodies and to face up to them better. Issues of age became irrelevant and all women taking the classes were able to come to terms with their looks, seeing through to their inner selves and inner beauty.

YOU SAY ...

EILEEN, 61: *I come from a long legacy of "I am ugly." I've had a bad body concept all my life. Before my exotic dancing experience, I could not see the beauty within me. I am articulate and 61 years young and can now speak triumphantly of my transformation. It was part of a process, a journey, that I undertook to claim parts of me that had either been buried or that I didn't know. I had to let go of the fear that has been pervasive in my life, and so I took the class for me! At this age, I wasn't going to be afraid to show my body.*

CAROLYN, 49: *I was looking to reconnect to life after beating death. Facing the task of bringing myself back into public was my motivation as I had survived breast cancer. At the point I signed up for the class, I had just finished six months of chemotherapy, surgery, and reconstruction therapy. I had just begun to get my hair back and move around again. I took the course to re-connect to my creative self within the real life force, the seat of power. I've been able to look at my body with more ease knowing I can love me. Whatever physical shape I'm in, I can be in my body again with more ease.*

Taking classes in the art of exotic dancing will do wonders for your body image and confidence. Relax and enjoy yourself when you are performing your dance and your partner will always appreciate your effort and careful thought.

Looking Good

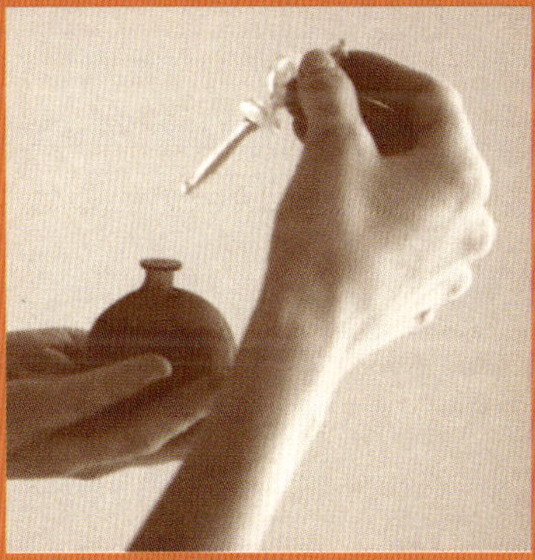

Setting the Scene

Find the time and energy to put on a dance for your partner. Make an effort to create a sensual atmosphere and take time out for yourself and your partner—it will leave you feeling both fulfilled and energized and the results will be well worth all your effort.

Create a great atmosphere. Start by tidying up your home. If the entire house is too much, clean up your dance room. Prepare your environment first and then take some time out for yourself—your mood sets the tone for your partner.

FLATTER YOUR SENSES

Establish a sensual atmosphere for your dance. First, create the environment you want through the use of lighting, sound, room temperature, and fragrance. To create a fun atmosphere, use a strobe or a lava lamp with background lighting. Achieve a sensual environment by using dimmed lights or go for the ultimate in romance by dancing to candlelight. Choose soothing and relaxing music to get your partner into the mood for your dance. Select similar music for your dance if you want the atmosphere to stay relaxed and sensual, or choose completely different music if you want to liven things up a bit. Be sure the temperature in the room is comfortable, and start with it cool since things are sure to get heated up quickly. Fragrance is the best aphrodisiac of all; scented candles calm the nervous

USE THESE APHRODISIAC FRAGRANCES

Jasmine: *stimulates hormone production and boosts creativity.* Patchouli: *increases sexual desire.* Rose: *boosts sexual confidence.* Sandalwood: *contains a substance described as the "raw fuel" of the libido.* Ylang ylang: *calms the body and mind and disperses stress and anxiety, both of which block sexual desire.*

system and are known aphrodisiacs (*see box, left*). Seductive fragrances are found in essential oils and scented candles. Certain aromas transmit messages to the limbic system in the brain, which houses your basic desires. Accessing these desires through the use of aphrodisiac oils and candles brings you closer to your goal of creating a relaxed and sensual environment. Use the seductive glow of candles as the final touches in creating your romantic sanctuary.

BE HAPPY!

It is important to create a fun, relaxed, comfortable, sensual, and safe environment for your partner and more importantly, for yourself. Your dance won't be much fun for your partner if you are so stressed out from organizing and planning that the only self-expression left to share is exhaustion, worry, and stress. To set the mood for yourself, indulge your own senses.

The ancient Greek verb "to bathe" also means to drive sadness from the mind. Relax with a sensual bath to unwind and free yourself up to enjoy this special time with your partner. Play music that makes you feel sensual and decide between a bubble bath, a sensual bath with essential oils, or detoxifying bath salts. Surround yourself by scented candles, set some fresh flowers in your bathroom, and smell them while in the bath. Choose fragrances that help to create the mood you want to achieve. Wrap up this luxurious time with fluffy bath towels and a special robe.

TRY MEDITATION

If meditation relaxes you, try your visualization exercises (*see p.62*) to get yourself in a frame of mind conducive to the environment you are trying to create. Lie down on your bed with soft lighting and subtle music and visualize scenes that help you feel relaxed. Don't fall asleep!

SPOIL YOURSELF

Treate yourself to a massage, facial, pedicure, or manicure. If you are one of the lucky few with lots of resources, treat yourself to all four. Pampering yourself is a great way to get re-energized and then you will have more to give your partner.

Creating your Style

Achieve your own personal style by accentuating your natural assets and keeping it simple. Having style does not mean making yourself look like someone else—this will only make you feel and look uncomfortable. And don't overdo it—just work with what you have and you will be surprised at the results of enhancing what is already there.

This section looks at three different areas of personal style: hair, make-up, and fashion. The instructions that follow are quite simple and there is a very good reason for that ... your styling should be simple!

MAKE THE MOST OF YOUR HAIR

Follow these guidelines for all hair types to achieve three easy different looks. **Recommended tools**: Seven- or nine-row flat brush; blow dryer with concentrator nozzle; straightening balm; pomade (soft gel) or wax; roller set; curling iron; flat iron; hairspray; mousse.

Straighten your naturally curly hair with a flat iron: divide it into four sections and run the iron smoothly down each length for a smooth, polished finish.

EXAMINE YOUR HAIRCUT

First of all review your hair cut. For styling purposes, the more proportional your hair is, the easier it is to handle. That basically means that the less layering you have, the easier a look is to achieve, even for those of you with fine or very straight hair. Add some low layering to create a flip, more bounce, and movement. Unless you are diligent about styling, layering will never be a friend.

CONDITION YOUR HAIR

Don't overlook the health of your hair. Condition your hair on a daily basis but don't insist on washing it each day. Shampoos contain detergents that clean your hair but also dry it out. When a shampoo claims to moisturize your hair, it is actually just using a less abrasive detergent. Volumizing shampoos use the strongest detergents of all. Long hair should be washed three times a week and conditioned every day. Always rinse your hair thoroughly to remove dirt, oil, and lingering odors from your scalp.

Creating your Style

A thick fall of hair in the peak of health is very attractive—condition regularly but do not wash your hair each day.

GO STRAIGHT

Although this style can be worn with any medium-to-long hair, it is easiest for those with straight hair. Wash, condition and, if necessary, use a straightening balm. Comb a small amount through your hair. If your hair is fine, leave a little conditioner in to help deal with tangles.

First dry your hair well. A brush will not style your hair until it is dry. Comb out any tangles and gently brush your hair, with the blow dryer directly overhead. If you have fine hair, you may only need to spend a minute or two on each section of hair, while others with thick or curly hair may need five-eight minutes per section.

Next use your flat iron. Divide your hair into four sections, two at the front on either side of the part, and two at the back. Run the flat iron slowly along from the hair shaft to the ends. After flat ironing each section, you should notice a considerable difference in your hair texture and thickness. Use a small amount of pomade or wax (just enough to to create a film over your palms) to finish the style. Place your hands on your scalp and run them down the length of your hair, pinching your fingers together at the end. This creates shine for your overall look and also adds volume to your hair.

WEAR A FULL MOON

Use a roller set for this style. Repeat the blow-dry process detailed as above but replace the flat iron with a roller set when your hair is dry. Add a light spray of gel to help the hair stick to the roller, part your hair wherever you want, and place the rollers in your hair horizontally away from the part, working down away from the part. Your hair should wrap about twice around the roller and generally the longer your hair, the larger roller you should use.

Once you've covered your entire head, spray hairspray or gel all over and let it sit for several minutes. Applying heat will accentuate the style, but is not necessary. Be sure to let your hair cool before removing the rollers as it is malleable when warm. Leave the rollers in for 15 minutes maximum and then remove them. Leave your curls as they are or brush them smooth for a neater look. Add hairspray for hold. If you have the time and the proper overhead dryer, use rollers on completely wet hair. This gives you a more defined curl and a strong, longer-lasting style. Comb your hair through with gel and place your rollers in as normal. It usually takes about 20-30 minutes for hair to dry under a dryer.

MAKE A PONYTAIL

Ponytails are very underrated but very easy to create. Use this lazy hair styling to your advantage—pig tails always look great on long hair and they are a great way to grab attention. Alternatively twist your ponytail into rope and wrap it around itself into a bun. Use a hair clip to hold it in place. It looks very sexy when you take out the clip and let your hair flow wildly over your shoulder!

DRESS UP SHORT HAIR

Let your hair settle and apply a good amount of pomade or strong-hold gel while it is wet. Take your hair dryer and dry it roughly. Don't be afraid to leave your hair in a slightly mussed-up style; let the wispy bits fall forward to frame your face and you will find yourself the hit of the show when you perform your dance.

SHARPEN UP YOUR COLOR

Follow the same basic rules when coloring your hair as when styling it. Less is more—keep it simple. For example, if you have black hair, do not go blonde. The bleach used will damage your hair dramatically, but most of all it just will not look right. You have a certain hair color for a reason, and it is this natural coloring that usually suits you best. Never lighten or darken your hair more than two-three shades from your natural color. If you feel that your hair needs livening up, try adding gold, red, natural brown, blonde tones, or highlights with semi-permanent hair color. The lighter your natural hair shade, the more color can be added. Avoid your roots showing—brown streaks on your scalp and bright blonde ends to your hair do not look attractive. Have your hair colored professionally and top it up once every couple of months to prevent dark roots from showing. Ask for streaks of natural color to prevent that over-done white-blonde look.

EXPERIMENT WITH MAKE-UP

Look for make-up that improves the condition of your skin while providing good coverage. Finding the right color and type of foundation, concealer, and powder is important to even out your skin and provide a clean canvas to accentuate your eyes, lips, and cheeks. Try a consultation in your local department store to find your base colors but remember these change with the seasons or vacation needs.

When it comes to blusher, different colors accomplish different looks. Your everyday look may find you using the correct colors for your skin tones so if you are going for a natural look, stick with those colors. If you are creating a new image, play with colors. For a sexy, sultry look, work in the bronzes, while a romantic look is achieved with reds. An innocent look incorporates pale pinks.

ACCENTUATE LIPS AND EYES

Lips and eyes are important when it comes to exotic dancing. Due to the emphasis on eye contact during your dance, spend time choosing the color and the image you want to convey. Romantic and innocent means light, bright colors, while sexy and sultry are achieved with smoky browns, grays, and plums. Match lipstick color to your blush color. Decide if you are going for innocent, sultry, or all-powerful. A bright red with a red lip liner is a strong, bold statement, while pale colors and glosses are all innocence and purity. Experiment, step out, and try something new. Try a look you always wanted to pull off. Go for it, you'll feel great.

PAINT YOUR NAILS

You use your hands all through your dance to trace your lines and guide your partner's eyes to where you want them, so make sure your nails look great. Have a manicure, or condition them with a softening scrub or cream treatment and then clip or file them into shape so they look neat. If your nails are short or bitten, choose a clear varnish to protect them; if you are happy with them, go crazy with wild, bright colors to match the image you are creating. Don't neglect your toe nails as you want your feet to look great in your sexy high heels!

If your nails are in great condition, go for deep colors to show them off. Tie in the shades you use with your make-up.

Choosing your Clothes

Styling is such a personal issue for most people, and even more so when it comes to deciding what to wear for your dance. Always wear clothing that is comfortable, because if you feel self-conscious or uncomfortable in an outfit, your performance will look both contrived and inhibited—not be much fun for you or your partner.

To feel good in your clothes you need to show off what you like best about your body. If that is your legs, then wear high heels and a short skirt, or high-cut shorts. If it is your chest, try a low-cut bra or bikini top. Your tummy? Then wear a figure-hugging cropped top. Remember that a striptease should be fun; if you are conservative with your hair and make-up, go to town on your clothes. Don't wear too much jewelry—a ring, necklace, and earrings are enough—anything more is just overkill!

THEME YOUR LOOK

Add a bit of playfulness into your dance by theming your look. Always dress in outfits that makes you feel desirable but never do anything or wear anything that makes you uneasy. Here are a few examples to get your imagination flying!

- **School Girl:** white shirt, plaid skirt, knee socks, pig tails ... you get the idea. Try something playful and fun. Scent the air with fresh smells to create an ambience of innocence. **Mindset:** Come play with me.

Dress to emphasize your good points and choose shoes that add to your theme—high, spiky heels always look sexy.

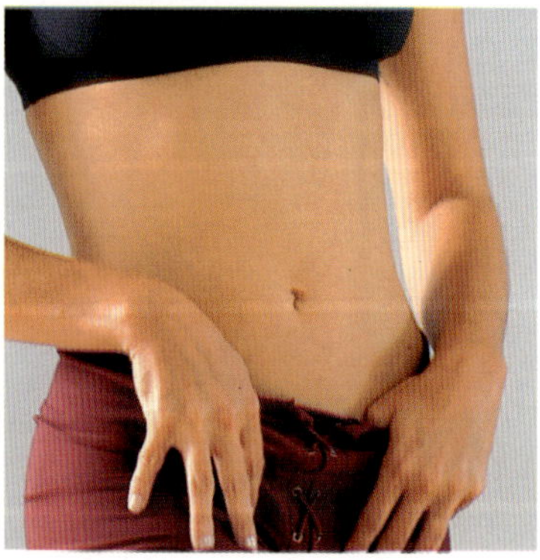

- **Cowgirl:** Frayed jeans or cut-off shorts, loose flannel shirt, hair down, and don't forget your hat, Faith Hill! **Mindset:** Yee-ha, good-time girl!

- **Jungle Jane:** Animal-print from a sexy little print dress à la Pebbles and Bam Bam to an oversized shirt with animal-print bra and G-string underneath. Choose music with a strong beat in it and if you can get your hands on a bear-skin rug, do it. Otherwise improvise with candles and a fluffy bath mat. **Mindset:** Wild animal stalking prey.

- **Dominatrix:** Leather, fishnets, handcuffs (even if only as a prop), black spiky heels, and a blindfold. Need we say more? **Mindset:** I'm in charge here.

Try playing nurse, teacher, secretary, or even the infamous stripper. Use your imagination, don't be afraid to experiment, and—above all—have fun!!

Choose fishnet stockings and elegant, silky accessories that feel sensuous and soft to the touch.

Stylish Shoes

The shoes! Everyone always wants to know about the shoes! Where do I buy them, how high do I go with the heels, and how the heck do I walk in stilettos? Bare feet are just fine, but heels will sex your whole image up and they also make your legs look great. Then again, don't wear any shoes that make you move awkwardly—that will spoil your whole performance.

For a sophisticated look, go with a closed-toe pump. Open-toed, strappy shoes are very sexy, while the classic "stripper" shoes are great for any of your themed outfits. To walk in your heels, keep your posture straight and maintain your balance. Step with the heel first, putting your weight onto the front of your foot. Practise so that when you dance, you feel comfortable and confident.

High, spiky heels make your legs look longer. Choose closed-toed pumps for elegance and strappy shoes for downright sexiness.

Index

Index

Discography

EXOTIC DANCING FAVORITES

Ashanti & JA Rule *Always on Time*

Mary J Blige *No More Drama*

Hot Chocolate *You Sexy Thing*

Joe Cocker *Leave your Hat On*

Robert Cray *Strong Persuader*

Celine Dion *A New Day*

Madonna *Erotica*

Melissa Etheridge *I'm the Only One*

Marvin Gaye *Sexual Healing*

Jimi Hendrix *Red House*

Faith Hill *Breathe*

Chris Isaacs *Bad Bad Thing*

Isley Brothers *Who's That Lady*

Janet Jackson *The Way Love Goes*

R Kelly *World's Greatest*

Alicia Keyes *Fallen*

BB King *Dangerous Mood*

Sarah McLaughlin *I Won't Fear Love*

Moby *Porcelain*

Nelly *Hot in Here*

Joan Osbourne *What if God Was One of Us*

Portishead *Glory Box*

Sade *Your Love is King*

Seal *Don't Cry*

Shaggy *Freaky Girl*

Shakira *Underneath your Clothes*

Brittany Spears *I'm A Slave for You*

Truth Hurts & Rakim *Addicted*

Santana *Supernatural*

Shania Twain *Feel Like a Woman*

Sting *Desert Rose*

U2 *Velvet Dress*

Usher *You Got It Bad*

On the Wild Side

Kid Rock *Cowboy*

George Thorogood *Bad to the Bone*

Warrant *Cherry Pie*

Def Leppard *Pour Some Sugar On Me*

For a Mature Audience

Peggy Lee *Fever*

Tom Jones *Ain't No Sunshine*

Tina Marie *Out On a Limb*

SOS Band *Tell Me If You Still Care*

Earth, Wind & Fire *Fantasy*

Alexander O'Neal *If You Were Here Tonight*

Harold Melvin & The Blue Notes *Wake Up Everybody*

LTD *Love Ballad*

Dane *Can't Fall Back*

Anything by: Luther Vandross, Barry White and Toni Braxton

VIDEOGRAPHY

AOED, The Art of Exotic Dancing for Everyday Women™, Core Moves

AOED, The Art of Exotic Dancing for Everyday Women™, Developing Your Own Routine

AOED, The Art of Exotic Dancing for Everyday Women™, Mood and Props

StripFit™—Total Workout

StripFit™—Abs

StripFit™—Bums and Thighs

Acknowledgments

This is much more than just a book to me. It is a symbol of the velocity and expansiveness of the breakthrough taking place in the realm of female sensuality. It is time for me to thank all the thousands of courageous women who have taken the class, tried the video, or picked up this book. You are expanding what it means to be a sensual woman and creating space for others to feel the joy of connecting to their authentic self. Without you, transformation is not possible. You are transformation.

Thanks to all our instructors now and in the future, and especially to my friends Tammy, Molly, and Coralissa as we embark on this journey together and share the common vision of transforming the face of female sensuality.

To Kathy Boccella, who unwittingly started this whole thing, and all the women from the first video, who are the real pioneers. To Lance Weiler and Barry Leshtz, who have helped move things along. To Cathie Miller for her unconditional belief in us and to Woody for his patience. To Chris Hooven for his beautiful home. To all those whose support allows our dream to expand: Tim's and my families and friends, Mr and Mrs MacElree, Bob and Yvonne Burns, Mary Drayton, Sigi and Caesar. To the Philadelphia Films and Learning Studio teams, thank you, and specifically to Karen for her typing.

To Carlton Publishing and their team (particularly Antonia and Sasha) for their hard work, and specifically to Judith More for her timely and clever decision to produce this book.

To Jules for his fabulous photos. To Lindley, who is so quick and smart and exceptional with words (I wish I had more time with you while writing this book, it would have been much better). You should be the writer. I can't wait to do marketing with you.

To Tim, my partner in everything I do. Without you there would be no book. Without you there would be no Learning Studio or Philadelphia Films. Thank you for your love, support, and generosity.

Leah Stauffer

Classes

For retreats and world-wide class schedules or to request a class in your area, log on to: *www.artofexoticdancing.com*

Join the Art of Exotic Dancing™ Community today!

A Touch Exotic merchandise also available.